FINDING YOUR WAY

Neil Champion

amicus

Published by Amicus
P.O. Box 1329
Mankato, MN 56002

Printed in the United States of America, at Corporate
Graphics in North Mankato, Minnesota.

Library of Congress Cataloging-in-Publication Data
Champion, Neil.
  Finding your way / by Neil Champion.
     p. cm. -- (Survive alive)
  Includes index.
  Summary: "Gives essential survival tips for navigation in the wild,
including using natural means such as the sun and stars and using
technology such as compasses and GPS receivers"--Provided by
publisher.
  ISBN 978-1-60753-038-1 (library binding)
  1. Wilderness survival--Juvenile literature. 2. Orienteering--Juvenile
literature. I. Title.
  GV200.5.C435 2011
  613.6'9--dc22

                    2009030888

Created by Appleseed Editions Ltd.
Designed and illustrated by Guy Callaby
Edited by Stephanie Turnbull
Picture research by Su Alexander

DAD0038
32010

9 8 7 6 5 4 3 2 1

Contents

Lost!

Imagine being lost in wild forest, deep jungle, remote mountains, or snowy Arctic plains. You're all alone and there's nobody to show you the way. Storm clouds are gathering and soon it will be dark. It's up to you to survive. How would you find your way to safety?

Can you imagine finding your way across vast stretches of Arctic ice like this one? There are no landmarks, and huge icy ridges often block your view. It's so windy that you can hardly lift your head to look around.

Finding North

One of the most obvious methods of finding your way is to use a map—but it isn't the only tool you can use to **navigate**. And even a map is no good if you don't learn basic survival skills.

The first thing you need to do is figure out which direction you are facing. For this you need a compass. A compass has a needle that always points north.

▶ *You can buy compasses in different shapes and sizes, but they all work in the same way.*

How a Compass Works

The Earth is like a huge **magnet**. The ends of the magnet are called the magnetic North and South Poles. A weak **magnetic current** flows between these two poles. This pulls, or attracts, anything magnetic to line up with the North and South Poles. A compass needle is magnetic and always points north because it is pulled toward the magnetic North Pole. You can read more about how to use a compass on pages 16 and 17.

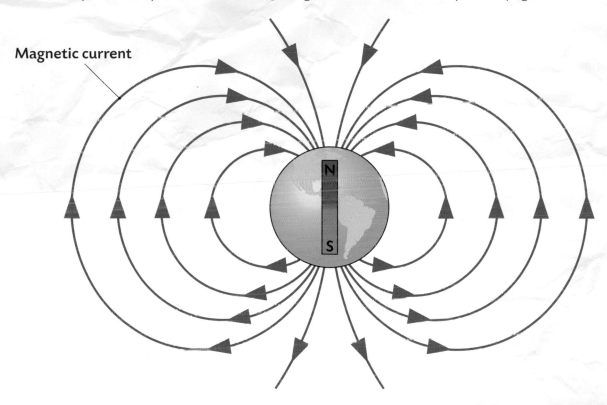

Magnetic current

Become a Navigator

Once you know where north is, you can start deciding which way to go. This book shows you all the key skills you need to become an expert navigator—**orienting** yourself, reading a map, taking **bearings**, using technology, using your head, and planning the best route to safety.

DID YOU KNOW?
The Earth's magnetic North and South Poles are not in exactly the same place as the geographical North and South Poles.

TRUE SURVIVAL STORY

DAN STEPHENS was a scout leader who took a group of scouts hiking in the woods in northern Minnesota in 1998. He left the group to explore alone and slipped on a patch of moss, hit his head, and lost consciousness. When he woke up, he was dazed and confused, and he managed to get completely lost. Fortunately he had excellent survival skills and knew how to use the sun and stars to navigate. Three days later he arrived safely back at his camp. This shows that good navigational skills could save your life—but also that you should always hike with other people, never alone.

Into the Unknown

People have wanted to find their way across unknown lands and seas for thousands of years. Some people were looking for new places to live, while others wanted to conquer rival tribes or kingdoms. Many explorers became rich and famous by discovering new places and trading with people who lived there. These adventurers had to know how to navigate, using the best technology from their age.

DID YOU KNOW?

Around 1,500 years ago, some Europeans thought the world was flat—so if you sailed too far, you'd drop off the end!

▶ *A famous explorer named Francis Drake sailed around the world from 1577 to 1580 in a ship called the* Golden Hinde. *This is a modern copy of his ship.*

Using Landmarks

Early explorers didn't have maps. They relied on their eyes and memory to find their way or retrace routes. Early sailors stayed within sight of the coastline when they traveled by sea. It wasn't always the quickest route, but it kept them from getting lost!

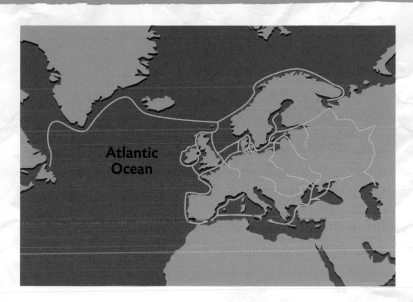

Atlantic Ocean

▶ *This map shows some of the routes taken by Viking sailors. You can see how they followed the coast whenever possible.*

The First Maps

The first accurate maps were made in Europe in the 1580s. Sailors used them to explore sea routes around the world. Countries such as Britain, Portugal, and Spain became great rivals in the race to conquer foreign lands. Maps were also important for explorers searching for gold, spices, and other treasures.

▲ *This map of South America comes from a Spanish atlas made in 1582.*

Modern Explorers

More recently, people have explored the world for scientific reasons, or to test themselves against extreme climates—for example, climbing mountains in remote, frozen lands, journeying to the North or South Pole, **trekking** through dense jungles, and crossing vast deserts.

TRUE SURVIVAL STORY

ROALD AMUNDSEN is famous for being the first person to reach the South Pole. He was also the first person to navigate along the Northwest Passage, a sea route through the Arctic Ocean. This was a difficult journey through drifting ice, and it got even worse when Amundsen's compass needle broke. The ship floated in thick fog and he was afraid it would hit a wall of ice. Then he felt the ship rock from side to side and knew they were safe. The rocking was caused by ocean waves, which meant they were nearly through the narrow Northwest Passage and would soon be out on open sea.

Ancient Skills

Navigators in ancient times used the world around them to find their way. They knew that plants, animals, and weather had regular patterns, and they learned to read these signs. The best thing about these ancient skills is that you can use them yourself when you're out in the wild.

Wind Direction

Wind usually blows from one particular direction. This is called the prevailing wind. Trees in exposed places grow away from the prevailing wind. If you know the direction of the wind, look at leaning trees to help figure out which way you're heading.

These trees in North Carolina are always blown in the same direction by a strong prevailing wind. Their trunks and branches lean away from the wind.

Sea birds usually fly close to land. Sailors look for birds as a clue that land is near.

Amazing Animals

Keep an eye out for animals, as many of them are good natural navigators. Animals that **migrate** can find their way across whole countries and oceans to reach nesting or breeding grounds. They use their senses of sight and smell, but scientists think they can also sense the Earth's magnetic currents and use them to navigate. If you know which way groups of migrating animals are heading, then you can use them to check your own position.

▼ *Polynesian sailors, like the men shown here, still use many traditional skills to find their way across the Pacific Ocean.*

TRUE SURVIVAL STORY

MAU PIAILUG is a Polynesian sailor who is skilled at navigating using ancient skills. In 1976, he and his crew set off to sail from Hawaii to Tahiti without any modern navigational aids. It was a big challenge, but Mau was sure that it could be done by using the sun, moon, and wind, as well as the pattern of waves on the ocean. They were at sea for a month and had to battle strong winds that threatened to blow them off course. Finally, Mau spotted a group of sea birds called terns skimming over the sea, so he knew land was near and the voyage had been a success.

Watching the Waves

In ancient times, sailors from Polynesian islands in the Pacific Ocean used waves to navigate between islands. By observing the direction of waves and how they rocked the boat, sailors knew which way to go. Polynesian navigators also tracked movements of stars, the direction birds were flying, and the position of clouds, which tend to cluster above islands rather than over the ocean.

Using the Sun

The sun is a very useful tool. It can help you find your way on land or at sea, as long as it isn't hidden by heavy clouds or fog. Wherever you are in the world, the sun rises in the east and sets in the west. In the **northern hemisphere**, the sun is **due** south around noon (due north in the **southern hemisphere**). But don't forget that this varies slightly over the year. In winter, the sun is lower in the sky than in summer, and is in the sky for less time.

If you walk toward the rising sun, you are heading east.

Make Your Own Shadow Stick Compass

You can use the sun to make a simple compass. This will work at any time of day, as long as the sun is shining. All you need is a stick and two pebbles.

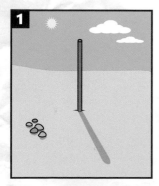 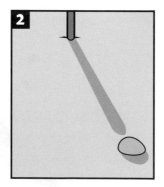 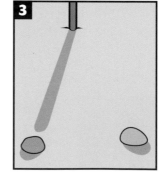 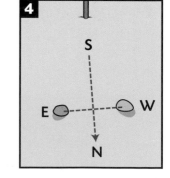

1. *Find some flat ground that isn't in the shade. Push a stick upright into the ground so that it casts a shadow.*

2. *Place a pebble at the end of the shadow cast by the stick.*

3. *Wait about 20 minutes, and then put another pebble at the end of the new shadow cast by the stick.*

4. *Mark a line in the ground between the two pebbles. This line points east and west. A line at **right angles** through the middle of this line points north and south.*

Telling the Time Using the Sun

You can turn a shadow stick compass into a very simple clock, or **sundial**, by marking the position of the shadow at each hour of the day. Sundials have existed since ancient times. Many plot very accurately the sun's course across the sky at different times of the year.

▶ *Stonehenge, in England, is like a giant clock. The stones are aligned with the sun as it rises in midsummer.*

TRUE SURVIVAL STORY

TAMI OLDHAM ASHCRAFT is a sailor who got caught in a tropical storm as she was sailing a yacht from Tahiti to San Diego. Ashcraft was knocked unconscious. When she woke up, the storm was over but her mast had snapped, and the engine and electronic equipment didn't work. Ashcraft spent two days using a sextant to work out her position, then plotted a route to Hawaii. She worked carefully, as one mistake in her calculations could leave her stranded at sea. Then she rigged up a sail and set off—and 42 days later she reached land. Her skill at using a sextant had saved her life.

DID YOU KNOW?
The world's biggest sundial is at Jaipur Observatory, in India. The post that casts shadows is 89 feet (27 m) high.

Sun and Sea

When sailors are out at sea, they use the position of the sun to calculate how far north or south they are. They do this with a complicated tool called a **sextant**. This tells them the **latitude** of their ship by lining up the **horizon** and the sun.

▶ *A sailor with a sextant. Sextants also work at night by using stars instead of the sun.*

Navigating at Night

Thousands of years ago, people noticed that stars in the night sky formed patterns. They made maps of the stars and named the patterns, or **constellations**. People also realized that they could use the position of certain constellations to help them navigate at night. It's a skill that you can learn to use too.

The North Star

In the northern hemisphere, there is one very bright star called the North Star or Pole Star. It is always positioned above the North Pole, which means that it can show you where north is. To find the North Star, first look for a constellation called the Big Dipper or the Great Bear.

1

1. These are the stars that make up the Big Dipper. If you imagine a line joining them, they form the shape of a cup with a long handle.

2. Now look for the two bright stars at the end of the cup shape.

The Big Dipper

3. Draw an imaginary line from those two stars and you will see the North Star.

4. Now draw an imaginary line from the North Star to the ground. This direction is north. Try to find a landmark on the ground to make it easier to remember. Now you also know that south is behind you, east is right, and west is left.

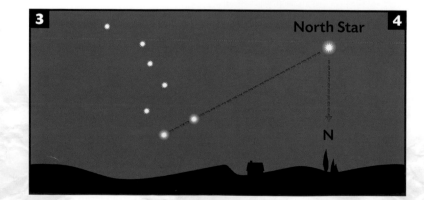

North Star

N

These campers in Vancouver, Canada, are studying constellations in the northern hemisphere using telescopes.

These are the stars that make up the Southern Cross. Can you see the cross shape?

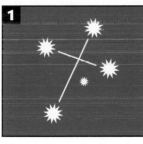

The Southern Cross

There are different constellations in the southern hemisphere. Unfortunately, there is no single bright star to tell you where south is. Instead, you can use a constellation called the Southern Cross.

1. *The Southern Cross has five stars. The four brightest stars make a cross shape.*

2. *Extend an imaginary line from the end of the cross. Make it four and a half times the length of the cross.*

3. *Now draw an imaginary line to the ground. This shows you where south is. Find a landmark to help you remember. Now you also know that north is behind you, east is left, and west is right.*

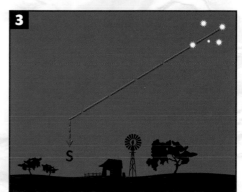

Reading a Map

Maps provide all kinds of information to help you navigate. They highlight features such as rivers, paths, and cliffs. They tell you the distance between these features and how high the land is. They also have symbols to show where landmarks are. To find all this information, you must know how to read maps.

◀ *This walker is using a special hiking map that shows useful details such as trails, paths, and campsites.*

▼ *These contour lines show two hills. The hill on the left must be steeper since the contours are closer together.*

Signs and Symbols

Take a good look at a map. Can you see the contours? These are lines that link land of identical height and therefore show where hills and valleys are. The closer together the contours are, the steeper the ground rises. Rivers are blue lines. Can you find the symbol for a bridge or any other feature that might cross a river? Get to know what paths and roads look like on maps. You can find all the features and symbols in the map's **key**.

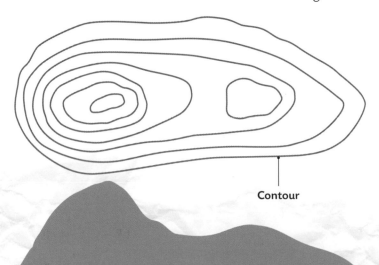

Contour

Grid Lines

Numbered grid lines run up and across a map and divide it into squares. Places listed in the map index have grid references to help you find which square they're in. A grid reference combines the numbers of the lines that cross in the bottom left-hand corner of the square. There is also a map **scale** that shows how much land each square represents.

◀ *This X has a grid reference of 16/57.*

Orienting a Map

To use your map, you have to orient it. This means lining it up with the land around you, so that the two match. First look around you. Pick out some obvious features, such as hills, paths, or a river. Now find them on your map. Turn the map in your hands until it matches the landscape. Sometimes you have to walk a little ways to spot an obvious feature that you can find on the map.

Remember, a map is only useful if you have an idea of where you are and where you need to go. You have to check your starting location, then keep checking your position as you walk.

▲ *In mountainous areas, you can get a good view of the surrounding land from a ridge like this one.*

TRUE SURVIVAL STORY

JASON RASMUSSEN set off on a three-day hiking trip in northern Minnesota in 2001. He had a map but didn't bother checking it—the trail looked easy to follow. As the trail faded out into dense woods, Rasmussen realized he was lost. He studied his map but couldn't figure out where he was. Not being able to find his campsite, he found shelter in a fallen tree trunk. He was finally rescued seven days later, but he had learned his lesson—keep checking your map!

Get Your Bearings

Explorers have used compasses for around a thousand years. The first compasses were very simple, but over time the design has been improved to give more accurate readings. Modern compasses can be very useful instruments in the wild, as long as you know how to read them properly.

DID YOU KNOW?
North on maps is in a slightly different place from the magnetic North Pole, which is where your compass arrow points. The difference between the two is called **magnetic variation**.

▲ *A compass works wherever you are in the world, in all weather conditions.*

Compass Design

In a modern compass, the magnetic needle sits in liquid inside a sealed case. The liquid protects the needle and stops it from wobbling or swinging too much. This makes it easier to read. The compass needle is luminous, so you can see it in the dark. Some very high quality compasses can be mounted on tripods, which gives an even more accurate reading.

Taking a Bearing

A bearing is the direction you need to go in to reach your destination. It's vital to know how to take a bearing using a compass and a map.

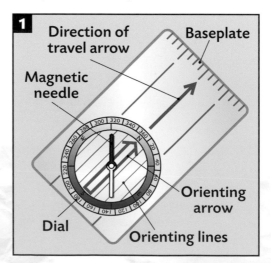

1 Direction of travel arrow · Baseplate · Magnetic needle · Orienting arrow · Dial · Orienting lines

1. *First, make sure you know the parts of your compass. The red half of the needle points north. The round dial shows directions and* **degrees**. *An orienting arrow and lines run across the dial. There is also a direction of travel arrow.*

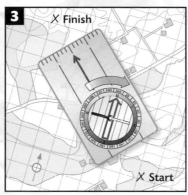

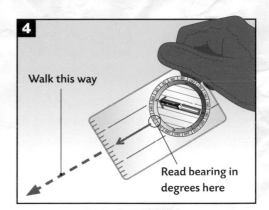

2. Now use a map to find where you are and where you want to go. Line up a compass between the two places, with the direction of travel arrow pointing where you want to go.

3. Turn the dial so that the orienting arrow points the same way as north on your map—this is usually the top of the map. Line up the orienting lines with the map's grid lines.

4. Turn the compass in your hands until the orienting arrow and the red side of the needle point the same way. The way the direction of travel arrow now points is the bearing to follow. The map key will tell you how to adjust this to allow for magnetic variation.

TRUE SURVIVAL STORY

ERIC LEMARQUE is a snowboarder who got lost in the Sierra Nevada mountains, in 2003. He was out in freezing conditions for seven days before he was rescued, and got very bad **frostbite**. He wasn't carrying any navigational equipment, but he was smart enough to know how to make his own compass. This showed him that he was walking in the wrong direction, so he used his homemade compass to get back on track and start heading nearer to civilization.

Make Your Own Compass

Now try making a simple compass of your own. You will need a small metal object, such as a needle.

1. Rub the needle in one direction against a magnet for about 30 seconds. This makes the needle magnetic.

2. Tie a piece of thread around the middle of the needle and hang it up so that the needle can turn freely.

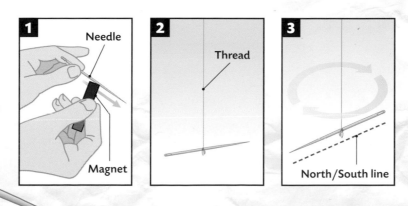

3. The magnetized needle will swing around to align itself with north and south. You can figure out which is which using your watch and the sun (see page 23).

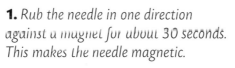

High-tech Gadgets

Today there are amazing pocket-sized gadgets that tell you exactly where you are, anywhere in the world. These handy tools are called GPS receivers and they work 24 hours a day, in all weather conditions. GPS stands for Global Positioning System. This system was created in the United States in the 1970s to help military forces navigate, but today anyone can buy and use GPS receivers.

◄ A walker uses a GPS receiver to check his location. Most GPS readings are accurate to around 33 feet (10 m).

TRUE SURVIVAL STORY

JEAN-LOUIS ETIENNE is a French doctor and explorer. In 1986, he set out from northern Canada to reach the North Pole on foot. It was very hard to navigate, as all he could see were huge ridges of ice. His main navigational tool was a radio transmitter that sent signals via satellite to his colleagues in France. They were able to see his position and send him instructions on where to go next. The system worked well and, after 63 days of walking, he reached the North Pole.

How GPS Works

1. *There are 24 GPS satellites in space at all times. Each satellite travels around Earth twice a day on its own fixed path. Satellites send out radio signals that can be picked up by GPS receivers.*

2. *A GPS receiver picks up signals from the nearest four satellites. It times how long the signals take to arrive and calculates its position on the Earth's surface.*

1

Satellite paths

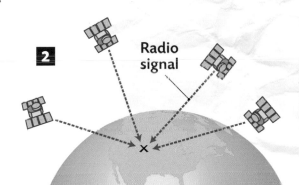

2

Radio signal

Taking a Reading

If you have a GPS receiver, make sure you key in the local time so that the receiver is operating in the right **time zone**. Now you can use it to pick up satellite signals and find your position. It can show your latitude and **longitude** or give you a grid reference to check on your map. It can also give details such as **altitude**.

◀ *Tall trees can block satellite signals. This makes GPS readings less accurate.*

Beware!

If you can't see the sky, then satellite signals may not reach you. Also, never forget that the receiver uses batteries. If they go dead, it will be no use at all. Finally, remember that a good navigator never relies on just one tool—carry a map and compass too, and observe your surroundings carefully. Then if your GPS receiver falls into a river, you won't panic!

DID YOU KNOW?
Batteries wear down much faster in cold weather. Remember this if you're using a GPS receiver in a cold place.

Danger!

Any outdoor adventure—whether it's a walking trip in the mountains or a rafting expedition down an unknown river—can go wrong if you get lost. You need to know where you are on the map and on the ground at all times. In poor visibility or hazardous territory, your navigational skills could save your life.

Be Prepared

Always be prepared for the level of adventure you are undertaking. Do you know how to navigate in the terrain? What's the weather forecast, and what difference might the weather make? What hazards are there? Study your map before you set off. There may be cliff edges close to the path, swampy areas, or large featureless regions where it may be hard to get your bearings.

Never hike alone in heavy mist or fog. Make sure you always stay with a group.

Stay Alert

Places like cliffs and bogs can be dangerous, especially in bad weather. You need to take very accurate bearings to plan a safe route, but don't walk along with your nose in a map! Pay attention to written warning signs and don't go anywhere that looks unsafe. Be aware of animal tracks and droppings to avoid disturbing wild animals.

You're Lost—What Now?

If you get lost, don't panic. Try to think clearly about what you have seen and walked past recently. Now look for these features on your map and trace your route until you can locate yourself. Can you see clues around you to help? If visibility is poor, explore your immediate surroundings using the method below.

1. First put a clearly visible object on the ground. Make sure it isn't something important, in case you lose it. Take a bearing north and count 100 paces. What do you see?

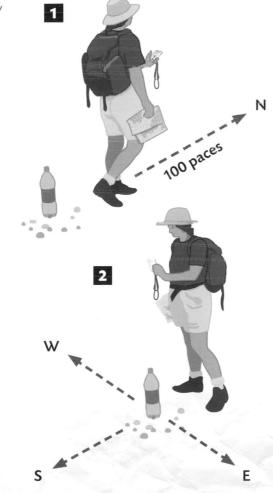

2. Take a bearing to your starting point and walk back. Now repeat the process, but walk west, then east, and finally south. This way you can build a picture of where you are and fit it to the map.

△ In areas where bears live, stick to clear paths or trails. Bears usually ignore humans, but in dense forest you might disturb one.

TRUE SURVIVAL STORY

BOYD SEVERSON is a hiker who set off to climb Mummy Mountain in Colorado. As he walked, he sent cell phone messages to a friend to stay in touch. Then a snowstorm set in. Severson got lost and realized his phone wasn't working. He spent the night outdoors and luckily was rescued in the morning. He knew he should have paid more attention to his surroundings instead of relying on his phone.

Smart Skills

Your map, compass, and GPS receiver are very important tools for navigating in the wild, but what if something unexpected happened and you were stranded without them? You would have to rely on other survival skills to stay alive. Here are a few handy hints and tips.

A sudden snowstorm like this one can make you lose your bearings.

Look for Clues

If you have no map, compass, or GPS receiver, don't just guess where to go. Try using some of the ancient skills you have learned in this book. For example, can you use the sun to figure out which direction you're facing?

Do you know which way the wind is blowing? Use all the clues you can find to piece together where you are. But beware—some signs are more reliable than others. For example, the sun is always regular, but wind can often change direction.

Use Your Watch to Find North and South

If the sun is shining and you're wearing a watch, you can use a clever trick to find north and south. You must have an analog watch, which means that it has hands to show the time.

1. *If you're in the northern hemisphere, point the hour hand of your watch as accurately as you can at the sun.*

2. *Now look for 12 o'clock on your watch. Imagine a line halfway between the hour hand and 12 o'clock. This line points south.*

3. *The position exactly opposite this line (180 degrees in the other direction) will point north.*

4. *In the southern hemisphere, point the 12 o'clock position at the sun. Imagine a line between 12 o'clock and the hour hand to find south.*

Plant Signs

Use plants around you to help find directions. Flowers usually face the sun, while **lichens** and mosses like to grow in the shade. In the northern hemisphere, this means they usually cover the north side of rocks and trees. The opposite is true in the southern hemisphere.

◀ *Moss can grow all over trees, but very thick, green moss like this is usually on the north side.*

The compass plant grows in central North America and gets its name because its leaves almost always face north and south. They do this to avoid the hot noon sun shining on them. You can use the leaves to help figure out which way you're facing.

Compass plant

TRUE SURVIVAL STORY

SEBASTIAN GOMEZ is a snowboarder who got lost in heavy snow in the mountains of New Mexico. He had no map, compass, or any other navigational tools. All he could do was try to make a shelter and hope rescuers would find him. He waited a whole night and all the next day. On the second night, he heard a rescue helicopter overhead. Desperate to attract its attention, Gomez had a smart idea. He held up his MP3 player and turned it on so that the screen lit up. The helicopter crew spotted the light and Gomez was saved. His quick thinking had saved his life.

Real-life Navigators

Many people around the world use navigational skills every day. This might be because they live in the wild and use traditional methods of finding their way. Or it might be because they navigate as part of their job—on land, at sea, or in the air.

Outback Trackers

Aborigines, or native Australians, are amazing navigators. They learn traditional ways of tracking animals and finding water in the vast Australian **outback**. In the past, explorers used Aboriginal trackers as guides. There is also a special unit in the Australian police made up of Aboriginal trackers. They help find criminals and rescue missing people.

▼ *Aborigines learn tracking skills at a very young age. This man is showing children how to follow animal tracks.*

On the Move

There are many groups of **nomads** around the world, particularly in Central Asia and Africa. Nomadic people travel long distances over difficult terrain such as deserts, herding animals to new grazing sites. They carry their tents and belongings with them and are skilled at finding their way and surviving in the wild.

A nomad leads camels across the Sahara Desert. Some nomads use cell phones to stay in touch with each other.

TRUE SURVIVAL STORY

ISAAC, JANE, AND FRANK DUFF were children from a poor shepherding family who lived in Victoria, Australia, in the 19th century. One day, their mother sent them out to collect twigs to make a broom. They got lost in dense bush and wandered, weak and scared, for nine days. Their family and friends searched for them, but rain had washed away their footprints. Finally the family asked an Aboriginal man named Woororal to help. Woororal was an expert tracker, and within a day, he and two helpers found the children alive.

Trained Navigators

Armed forces around the world use trained navigators called pathfinders. These are paratroopers who locate, set up, and equip areas of land for military operations.

Other trained navigators include guides who take people backpacking in mountains and deserts. They need to know how to navigate to a very high standard, because other people's lives depend on them. Mountaineering guides train for an average of five years.

Out and About

The best way of becoming a good navigator is to get out and practice your skills, even if it's just in your backyard. You could also join a group that provides navigating activities, such as orienteering, climbing, sailing, or camping.

Orienteering

Orienteering is a sport in which you have to find a series of fixed markers, using a map and compass to navigate. The courses can be long or short, hard or easy, and in all kinds of terrain. Everyone starts at a different time, so you can't follow the person in front!

1. *You are given a map at the starting point. Circles show where markers are and the order they must be visited in. You also have a card with a numbered box for each marker.*

2. *Using the map and a compass, decide the best route to take.*

3. *Markers are white and orange flags. To show that you have found one, punch your card with the special hole punch attached to the marker.*

Find Your Way . . . Fast

Many experienced navigators take part in the World Orienteering Championships, which are held every year in a different country. There are many events, including sprints, long-distance races, and relays for three-person teams. Competitors have to be expert map-readers to find the best route through unknown terrain—and fast runners to get around it quickly.

▼ *In orienteering races, all the competitors start at the same time but often take different routes to the finish line.*

Things to Do Outside

Take a compass outside and practice finding north. Study the natural landscape—can you see moss growing on trees? Find out where the local prevailing wind comes from, or work it out by making a note of where the wind blows from over seven days. This may also help you notice changes in wind direction.

Ask an Expert

You can also take navigating lessons from experts. Mountaineering instructors show groups of people how to find their way in the mountains. This includes navigating over large distances and also moving accurately over very small areas. These skills are vital when the weather is bad and one wrong move could be fatal.

Test Your Survival Skills

Now it's time to test your navigating knowledge! Can you remember all the things you've learned in this book? Have you got what it takes to find your way in the wild? You can find the answers on page 32.

1. Which of these sentences is true?
a) The sun rises in the west and sets in the east.
b) The sun rises in a slightly different direction each day.
c) The sun rises in the east and sets in the west.
d) The direction in which the sun rises depends on which hemisphere you're in.

2. If you're walking with the setting sun on your left, which way are you heading?
a) North
b) East
c) South
d) West

3. Which of these natural navigation aids is the most reliable?
a) Stars
b) Wind
c) Birds
d) Moss

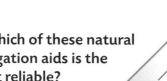

4. On a compass, what are the orienting lines used for?
a) To check you've got the compass the right way up.
b) To help you line up the compass with grid lines on your map.
c) Nothing, they're just decoration.
d) To help you figure out which way is north.

5. Which of these sets of contour lines matches the hill at the bottom of the page?

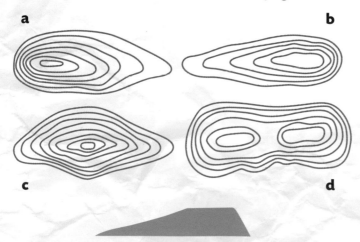

a

b

c

d

6. What does GPS stand for?
a) Guided Pocket Satellite
b) General Purpose Signaller
c) Geo-Planetary Service
d) Global Positioning System

7. You're hiking when a storm begins. Fortunately, you find a cave for shelter. It's too dark to read your map, so you use your GPS receiver to check where you are. Why might it not work properly?
a) It's too dark.
b) GPS satellites don't operate during stormy weather.
c) The cave roof may be blocking satellite signals.
d) The receiver may have gotten damp.

8. Which of these things DOESN'T happen in a whiteout?
a) You lose your sense of direction.
b) Your compass stops working.
c) You can't tell whether things are near or far away.
d) You can't see the horizon.

9. You realize you're completely lost in the wilderness. What's the first thing you should do?
a) Run, jump about, shout—anything to attract attention.
b) Turn around and go back the way you think you came.
c) Climb the highest hill you can find and have a look around.
d) Stop, keep calm, and try to think clearly about where you are.

10. What are sastrugi?
a) Ridges in the snow formed by wind.
b) Nomadic herdsmen who navigate using the sun.
c) Special markings on a sextant.
d) Contour lines that show very high mountains.

11. What do you need to make your own compass?
a) A stick, a watch, and a map.
b) A magnet, a needle, and thread.
c) A battery, a watch, and the sun.
d) A pen, paper, and a magnet.

12. Using the stars, can you work out which of these points is north?

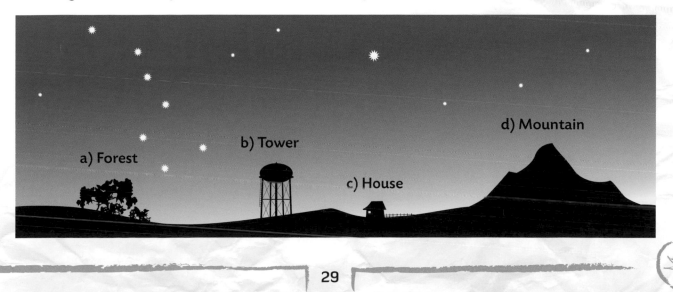

a) Forest
b) Tower
c) House
d) Mountain

Glossary

altitude How high you are.

bearings Your position in relation to other things. It can be hard to get your bearings in bad weather when you can't see clearly.

constellation A group of stars that form a pattern. There are 88 constellations.

degree A unit of measurement that is used when taking a compass bearing. There are 360 degrees around a compass dial. In the northern hemisphere, north is at 0/360 degrees, east at 90 degrees, south at 180 degrees, and west at 270 degrees.

due Exactly or directly.

frostbite A painful medical condition in which skin and other tissue in the human body is damaged because of extreme cold.

grid reference A specific location on a map, defined by coordinates on the map going across and up.

horizon The line in the distance where the land and sky seem to meet.

key A list that explains the symbols and signs on a map. It is often in a box at the side of the map.

latitude A measurement of how far north or south a place is from an imaginary line called the equator, which runs around the middle of the world.

lichen A living thing that grows on places such as tree trunks and bare ground. Lichens can look like crusty patches or bushy growths.

longitude A measurement of how far east or west a place is from an imaginary line called the Prime Meridian. This runs down the world from north to south and passes through Greenwich in England.

magnet An object that has an invisible force that pulls iron or steel toward it. The ends of a magnet are called poles.

magnetic current An invisible force that always flows in a fixed direction, between the two poles of a magnet.

magnetic variation The slight difference, measured in degrees, between grid north on your map and magnetic north on your compass. It varies depending on where you are in the world. You need to add or subtract the magnetic variation to take completely accurate bearings.

migrate To move to a different place to live.

navigate To work out your position or plan a route from one place to another.

nomad A member of a tribe or group who moves from place to place with herds of animals.

northern hemisphere The northern half of the world. It is separated from the southern hemisphere by an imaginary line around the middle of the world called the equator.

orient To figure out where you are in relation to your surroundings.

outback The vast, dry wilderness that covers large parts of Australia.

right angle The space between two connected lines that measures 90 degrees. Right angles are formed when a vertical, or upright, line crosses a horizontal, or level, line.

sastrugi Long grooves or ridges in snow, made by the wind. Each groove is called a sastruga.

satellite An object that travels around a planet. Many satellites are built to do certain jobs, for example to send radio signals to GPS receivers.

scale The size of a map in relation to the area it shows, for example 1 in.=0.5 mile. Some scales appear as ratios, such as 1:25,000, where 1 cm on the map represents 25,000 cm (or 250 meters) of land. Other maps have a scale bar, which is a line with measurements marked on it.

sextant A tool for navigating that is made up of a telescope and measuring equipment. Sailors can figure out their location by using a sextant to calculate the position of the sun, moon, or stars above the horizon.

southern hemisphere The southern half of the world. It is separated from the northern hemisphere by an imaginary line around the middle of the world called the equator.

sundial A device that shows the time on sunny days. A fixed upright object casts a shadow onto a surface that has hours marked on it.

time zone A region that has one particular time. The Earth is divided into different time zones. If you travel to a new time zone, you must change your watch to the time in that zone.

trekking Similar to backpacking. Hiking through mountainous or other wilderness areas; trekking journeys often last several days and include camping overnight.

whiteout A condition in snowy places where a blizzard combined with thick, white cloud cover and snow on the ground makes everything a confusing blur of white.

Useful Web Sites

http://home.howstuffworks.com/ camping-safety-tips-for-kids4.htm
Simple description of how to use a compass while camping.

www.wilderness-survival.net/chp18.php
Navigation and survival training information taken from the U.S. Army survival manual.

www.wilderness-survival-skills.com/ finding-direction.html
Practice finding directions using ancient skills.

www.abc-of-hiking.com/navigation-skills
Find plenty of helpful information on all the navigational skills you need to go hiking.

Index

Answers to survival skills quiz (pages 28–29)

1 c, 2 a, 3 a, 4 b, 5 b, 6 d, 7 c, 8 b, 9 d, 10 a, 11 b, 12 c